Movement in Steady Beat

Other movement and dance materials
by Phyllis S. Weikart*

BOOKS

Movement Plus Music: Activities for Children Ages 3 to 7, 2nd ed.

Movement Plus Rhymes, Songs, & Singing Games: Activities for Children Ages 3 to 7

Round the Circle: Key Experiences in Movement for Children

Teaching Movement & Dance: A Sequential Approach to Rhythmic Movement, 3rd ed.

Dance Notations to Accompany *Teaching Movement & Dance: A Sequential Approach to Rhythmic Movement* (set of cards)

Teaching Movement & Dance: Intermediate Folk Dance

RECORD/CASSETTE SERIES

Rhythmically Moving
(record series, also available in cassettes, compact discs)

Changing Directions
(record series, also available in cassettes)

VIDEOTAPES

Fitness Over 50
Beginning Folk Dances Illustrated

AUDIO TAPE

Rhythmically Walking

*Available from the High/Scope Press, 600 North River Street, Ypsilanti, Michigan 48198, (313)485-2000, FAX (313)485-0704.

THE HIGH/SCOPE® PRESS
A division of the
High/Scope® Educational Research Foundation
600 North River Street, Ypsilanti, Michigan 48198

Movement in Steady Beat

Activities for Children Ages 3–7

Phyllis S. Weikart

High/Scope Movement and Dance Consultant
Associate Professor, Division of Physical Education
The University of Michigan

with

Beverly Boardman
Helen Johnson
Judy Johnson
David Lipps
Gerry Miller
Richard Shivers
Connie Wright

Endorsed Trainers in Phyllis S. Weikart's
Rhythmic Movement and Folk Dance Curriculum

THE HIGH/SCOPE® PRESS

Published by
THE HIGH/SCOPE® PRESS
A division of the
High/Scope® Educational Research Foundation
600 North River Street
Ypsilanti, Michigan 48198
(313)485-2000, FAX (313)485-0704

Library of Congress Cataloging in Publication Data: LC-90-31138

ISBN 0-929816-08-0

Printed in the United States of America

10 9 8 7 6 5 4 3 2

Contents

Preface

*T*his booklet, and the two booklets that precede it, *Movement Plus Music* and *Movement Plus Rhymes, Songs, & Singing Games*, supplement my basic texts, *Round the Circle: Key Experiences in Movement for Children* and the third edition (1989) of *Teaching Movement & Dance: A Sequential Approach to Rhythmic Movement.*

The movement ideas presented in the three supplementary *Movement . . .* booklets are based on familiar rhymes and songs and can be used with the *Rhythmically Moving* series of records/cassettes. The booklets contain activities designed for use with children aged 3–7, but many of the activities can be tailored to meet the needs of older children as well.

In writing this booklet, I was assisted by seven others who are endorsed in my Rhythmic Movement and Folk Dance Curriculum. For their assistance with this project, I am very grateful to Endorsed Trainers Beverly Boardman, Bradenton, Florida; Helen Johnson, Dana, Indiana; Judy Johnson, Chico, California; David Lipps, Battle Creek, Michigan; Gerry Miller, London, England; Richard Shivers, Lawrenceville, Georgia; and Connie Wright, Duluth, Georgia.

Phyllis S. Weikart

How to Use This Booklet

*I*n *Round the Circle: Key Experiences in Movement for Young Children*, eight **key experiences in movement** are introduced: (1) Following Movement Directions, (2) Describing Movement, (3) Moving the Body in Nonlocomotor Ways, (4) Moving the Body in Locomotor Ways, (5) Moving With Objects, (6) Expressing Creativity in Movement, (7) Feeling and Expressing Beat, and (8) Moving With Others to a Common Beat. A ninth key experience, Moving the Body in Integrated Ways, is introduced in the third edition of *Teaching Movement and Dance*. This key experience is more suited to older children and adults.

In this booklet, we focus exclusively on the key experience **Feeling and Expressing Beat**. Youngsters who can feel and express beat possess **basic timing**, a fundamental skill that should be acquired before children enter elementary school. Being skilled in basic timing means (1) possessing *beat awareness* (being able to accurately feel and indicate beat in nonlocomotor ways) and (2) possessing *beat competency* (being able to match the beat by walking to it). From my 30 years of experience, I believe mastering basic timing at an early age gives children a head start in at least three important areas of development in the elementary grades: (1) **motor skills**, (2) **musical skills**, and (3) **academic skills**.

You will see that the activities presented in this booklet are divided into two categories—**rhymes** and **action songs**—and that appropriate age-ranges are specified. My approach to introducing movement and music activities to beginners of any age involves **active learning** experiences. An emphasis on active learning experiences is part of the High/Scope Foundation's developmental approach to educating children and youths. (For information on the High/Scope Curriculum, see *Young Children in Action: A Manual for Preschool Educators*.) To facilitate active learning, I recommend that during movement and music activities, you frequently encourage the children to lead the group, create their own verses, or choose other ways to move; as much as possible, children should make their own choices and decisions. Notice that to increase the opportunities for active learning experiences, we have altered the traditional words to many of the familiar rhymes and songs used in this booklet. Also, those familiar with the High/Scope Curriculum will recognize that in addition to incorporating some of the active learning key experiences, each of the activities in this booklet involves several of the other High/Scope key experience areas: language, representation, classification, seriation, number, spatial relations, and time.

Here are some suggestions to help you become familiar with each activity:

1. Note the intended **Age-range** for the activity. You may be able to modify the activity, if necessary, to suit the age-range of your group of children.

2. Review the **Equipment** section. In some of the activities, children work with props. Since young children may become frustrated if they have to share equipment, make sure there is enough equipment so that each child has a prop, or make suitable substitutions.

3. Review the **Formation** section. Is your activity area large enough to accommodate the movements, or do you need to modify the activity to fit your space? For example, if the activity calls for children walking around the room, but there is not enough space to do this, children can march in place instead. For activities that involve a circle formation, be sure to provide a "concrete" circle for the children (for example, you could make a circle on the floor with tape).

4. Read through the **Procedure** section, so you understand the movement sequence thoroughly before you present it to the children.

The Teaching Model

Keep in mind three ideas as you present the movement activities: **separate**, **simplify**, and **facilitate**.

Separate. When beginning an activity, separate what you say from what you do. For example, if the children are seated, and you want them to pat their ankles with both hands at the same time, you might say "Watch my hands and do what I do." Then, without talking, demonstrate the movement.

Simplify. If your goal is having the children pat both hands on their ankles, repeatedly, begin by placing both your hands on your ankles, and hold them there while the children copy your movement. Then slowly pat your ankles. By doing this you create a simple starting point.

Facilitate. Once the children have watched your demonstration or have performed a movement, help them develop a deeper awareness of the movement by asking such specific questions as "What body part are you patting? Are your pats fast or slow? Are they hard pats or soft pats?" To encourage children to be *active* participants in the learning process, also ask them open-ended questions that solicit their suggestions and ideas, and respond positively to this input.

Teaching Strategies: Achieving Success With Feeling and Expressing a Steady Beat*

• To assure children's success with each activity, you can emphasize the beat by using an **anchor word** that matches the movement. We recommend the following

---

*For a complete description of teaching strategies for presenting movement activities to young children, please refer to *Round the Circle: Key Experiences in Movement for Children*, and *Teaching Movement & Dance: A Sequential Approach to Rhythmic Movement*, both of which are available from the High/Scope Press.

start-up sequence: (1) As you start a movement, such as patting the knees, do not insist that everyone do it in exactly the same manner. (2) After everyone has tried the movement, establish a beat for the movement by using an anchor word such as "KNEES" and repeating this anchor word four or eight times. (3) Once you have used the anchor word to establish the beat, begin the rhyme or song.

• At first, select the rhymes and songs you are most comfortable with. Also, begin with activities that require children to stay in their own spaces rather than to move all about the designated activity area. For example, such an activity might require a child to march, jump, or hop, but only within the area defined by a carpet square or a hula hoop.

• When presenting beat activities in which children must alternate their hand or foot movements, do not expect them to understand the directions "right" or "left." Allow the children to decide which side they want to start with. You can say, for example, "one side" and "the other side," or "the first side" and "the second side."

• If a child is leading an activity, match the anchor word and the beat of the rhyme or song to the child's beat as you and the children sing or chant the rhyme together to accompany the movement.

• If the rhyme or song has more than one verse, stop between verses to re-establish the beat with the anchor word.

• When the children are using two hands at the same time to perform a beat, try to use beats of longer duration performed slowly rather than beats of shorter duration performed quickly.

• When using recorded music, try to set a beat for the movement that is as close as possible to that of the recording.

• To encourage children to sing, try to pitch the song higher than you would for adults. Adults frequently pitch songs too low for children.

• Add the rhyme or song (or phrases of the rhyme or song) only after all the children fully understand how to do the movement.

• Begin the rhyme or song immediately after you have chanted the anchor word. A pause will only confuse the children.

Rhymes

Aka Backa Soda Cracker

*Aka backa **so**da cracker,*
*Aka backa **boo**;*
*Aka backa **so**da cracker,*
***Pass** to **you**.*

Category

Rhyme

Age

6–7

Equipment

One soft ball or bean bag for each child

Formation

Ask the children to sit in a circle.

Procedure

Have the children practice saying "Pass to you." Ask them to make believe they are each passing a bean bag or soft ball to the lap of the next person in the circle when they hear the word "PASS." As you explain this procedure, rather than talking about passing to "the person on your right," *model* which way the object is to be passed (to the right or left), saying "Pass the bean bags this way." Next, begin a slow beat on your legs, saying "PAT" four times, and then add the rhyme. After asking the children to listen for the word "PASS" in the rhyme, repeat the rhyme, and have the children pretend they are passing their bean bags to their neighbors when they hear "PASS." After this practice, give the children their bean bags, and demonstrate how they can keep the beat by patting their bean bags on their laps. Remind them that on the word "PASS," everyone should pass bean bags. Finally, start the patting and the rhyme again, this time with everyone patting and actually passing a bean bag.

Variation

Have the children jump, hop, or walk (instead of patting) to the beat of the rhyme. Change the last line to "We (jump, hop, walk) with you." Or, for young children, change the last line to "How are you?" or "I like you." Ask the children for other suggestions for the rhyming last line.

Apples, Peaches, Pears, and Plums

*Apples, peaches, **pears**, and plums,*
***Tell** me when your **birth**day comes,*
(here supply a child's name).

Category

Rhyme

Age

5–7

Equipment

None

Formation

Have the children sit or stand around the area.

Procedure

Begin by talking with the children about which months their birthdays are in. Then explain that you are going to pat the beat while you recite a rhyme that asks them to tell their birthday months. When the rhyme asks a child his or her birthday month, that child can show a new way to begin patting the beat (on the knees or shoulders, for example.)

Begin the beat by having all the children copy you as you pat your face slowly and softly with both hands. Say the anchor word "BEAT" four times, and then add the rhyme, ending by asking for one child's birthday month. After the first child names a month and chooses a new place for everyone to pat the beat, repeat the rhyme and end with another child's name. Continue until everyone has had a chance to choose a way to pat the beat.

Variation

After saying the rhyme, proceed through all the months, saying each one four times while patting the beat.

January, January, January, January

When a child's month is said, that child stands and freezes into a statue shape.

Boys and Girls Went Out to Play,

Boys and girls went out to play,
Side to side they did sway.

Category

Rhyme

Age

4–7

Equipment

None

Formation

Ask the children to stand in a circle formation.

Procedure

Ask the children to show you how to sway, or how to move "side to side." Start swaying to a beat, using the anchor word "SWAY, SWAY." Encourage the children to describe how it feels to move in this way. Start the group swaying together by using the anchor words to establish a common beat. Add the rhyme. Ask the children to explore other ways to sway, such as bending backward and forward. Substitute words in the rhyme that describe the way the group is swaying. For example:

Boys and girls went out to play,
All together they did sway.

or

Back and forth they did sway.

Bubble Gum

*Bubble gum, **bub**ble gum, **chew** and **blow**,*
*Bub**ble gum, bub**ble gum, **scrape** your **toe**;*
*Bub**ble gum, bub**ble gum, **tastes** so **sweet**,*
***Get** that **bub**ble gum **off** your **feet**.*

Category

Rhyme

Age

6–7

Equipment

For each child, a stretch band, (made of about 3 ft of 1 ½-in. elastic formed into a loop)

Formation

Have the children spread out, with each one standing inside a circle formed by the stretch band.

Procedure

Encourage the children to actively explore what can be done with the bands. As they do so, describe what individual children are doing: "Davey, you're standing on your stretch band and pulling it up over your head. Meghan, you're using your legs to stretch the band." Now ask the children to stand on their stretch bands and to find ways to stretch the bands up and down without letting go of them. Encourage them to try stretching their bands using both hands, using just one hand, and using one hand and then the other hand. Begin using the anchor words "UP, DOWN" to establish the common beat for stretching the bands up and down, and then add the rhyme. Substitute words in the rhyme that describe the way the children are stretching the bands.

Variation

Ask the children to show you how they would walk (without using the bands) if they had bubble gum on the soles of their shoes. Encourage them to describe their movements. Repeat "WALK" four times to establish a group beat for these movements, and then add the rhyme. Finally, do the entire rhyme with the movement. You might also ask the children to think of other ways to move with the stretch bands (such as moving with a partner or walking in different ways).

Chocolate, Vanilla

Chocolate, vanilla, **take** *a* **scoop**;
Keep *the* **beat** *inside your* **hoop**.

Category

Rhyme

Age

4–7

Equipment

One hula hoop for each child (or for every 2–3 children)

Formation

Children may choose to stand either inside or outside their own hoops.

Procedure

First, explore spatial awareness terms with the children by discussing where they've chosen to stand. For example, ask individual children to describe where their feet are (whether inside or outside their hoops). Or say "Let's all stand inside our own hoops the way Maxwell is standing. Oh, Sara is standing beside her hoop; let's all try that. Tina is jumping outside her hoop; let's do it her way. Let's walk around our hoops as Mary is doing."

Next, ask the children to remain inside their hoops and to find a way to keep the beat while doing so. You could say "Jennie is bouncing inside her hoop; let's all bounce to keep the beat." Anchor the beat by saying "BEAT" four or eight times, and then add the rhyme. Ask the children to suggest other ways they can use hoops to move to the beat. The children might also think of other ice cream flavors to use in the rhyme.

Diddley Diddley Dumpty

Diddley diddley dump-ty,
The cat ran up the plum tree;
Half a crown to fetch her down,
Diddley diddley dump-ty.

The cat, the cat,
The diddley diddley cat;
The cat ran up the tree
O' Fiddley diddley dee.

Category

Rhyme

Age

5–7

Equipment

None

Formation

Ask the children to sit on the floor.

Procedure

Have the children explore ways to alternate hand movements in patting their hands on their legs. Say the anchor word "PAT" eight times to establish the beat for patting, and say the first verse of the rhyme. Then, have the children use both hands to touch their knees, waist, shoulders, and head in sequence, two times each. Have them say "KNEES, KNEES, WAIST, WAIST, SHOULDERS, SHOULDERS, HEAD, HEAD" as they perform the motions. Add the second verse of the rhyme when the children are comfortable with this.

Feeling Beat

*Brian wants to **know** your name;*
*Feeling beat is the **name** of the game.*
***Won't** you please tell **him** your name?*

Category

Rhyme

Age

3–7

Equipment

A stuffed animal or doll

Formation

Have the children sit in a circle.

Procedure

Introduce the stuffed animal or doll to the children (give it a name such as Brian), and explain that Brian likes to meet people. Go around the circle and ask the children to tell Brian their names. Then ask for a volunteer to be the one to help Brian feel the beat. The child holds Brian and chooses a part of him on which to pat the beat. Ask the other children to imitate what Brian is doing. Anchor the beat by saying "PAT" four times slowly, and then add the rhyme.

Footprints

*Little **feet**, little **feet***
***Walk** along this **little street**.*
Walk** up**on** your **own** path**way
***On** this **bright** and **sunny day**.*

Category

Rhyme

Age

5–7

Equipment

Vinyl or laminated construction-paper "footprints" created by the children (enough to provide each child with eight footprints)

Formation

Ask the children to stand scattered around the area.

Procedure

First have the children explore walking in different pathways—straight, curved, or zigzag. Then ask each child to use eight footprints to make some kind of pathway on the floor; encourage them to vary their pathways and to think of how they might fasten the footprints to the floor. Have the children try walking on their own pathways and then on other children's pathways.

After the pathways have been made and fully explored by the children, ask each child to choose a pathway and to stand at its beginning. You can set the beat by saying "WALK" four or eight times as each child walks in place at the beginning of his or her pathway. Then add the rhyme, and have children walk to the beat of the rhyme, following the footprints in their pathways. For the third line of the rhyme, use any word that describes a particular child's pathway.

Jack and Jill

Jack and *Jill* went **up** the **hill**
To **fetch** a **pail** of **wa–ter**.
Jack fell **down** and **broke** his **crown**,
And *Jill* came **tum**bling **af–ter**.

Up Jack **got** and **home** did **trot**
As **fast** as **he** could **ca–per**.
He **went** to **bed** to **mend** his **head**
With **vinegar** and brown **pa–per**.

Category

Rhyme

Age

6–7

Equipment

For each child, a capped plastic milk jug partially filled with water that's tinted with blue food coloring

Formation

Ask the children to spread out around the area.

Procedure

Swing your arms as though you were swinging two pails of water, and ask the children to watch what you're doing and to describe the movement. Next have everyone try swinging their arms in this way (do not use jugs for this). Repeat this sequence, this time swinging only one arm at a time. Anchor the beat for the arm-swinging by saying "SWING" four or eight times, and then say the rhyme. Once the children have mastered this, have them each practice swinging a jug back and forth with one arm. Encourage them to talk about the motion and the sound the water makes in the jug: "What does it sound like when you swing your jug?" Now repeat the anchor word again and add the rhyme, as the children swing jugs to the beat.

Jumping Joan

Here I am little jumping Joan.
When no one's with me, I'm all alone.

Here I am, little jumping Jack.
I jump to the middle, and then I jump back.

Here I am, little jumping Rose.
Jump right in, and hold that pose.

Here I am, little tiptoeing Carol.
I tiptoe around that great big barrel.

Here I am, little hopping Sue.
As I hop, you join me too.

Here I am, little marching Paul.
First I march short, and then I march tall.

Here I am with a beat so neat.
I'm going to rock it on my seat (feet).

Here I am with a real soft (loud) beat.
I'm going to keep it with my feet.

Category

Rhyme

Age

5–7

Equipment

None

Formation

Have the children stand about the area.

Procedure

Ask the children to try jumping in place. Set the beat by saying "JUMP" four or eight times, and then add the rhyme.

After this, encourage the children to try other ways of moving in place, and ask them to describe how they are moving (hopping, marching, tiptoeing). "Julie, you are hopping very fast. Kathryn, how are you moving?" Refer to the other verses for additional ideas, and encourage the children to make up verses.

Mary Mack

*Mary Mack **dressed** in black,*
*Silver buttons **down** her back.*
***Hi**-o, **hi**-o,*
***Hi**-o, hi-o, **hi**-o.*

Category

Rhyme

Age

3–7

Equipment

None

Formation

Ask the children to sit in a circle.

Procedure

Demonstrate tapping your shoulders with both hands at the same time, and ask the children to do the same thing. As you tap your shoulders along with the children, establish the beat by saying "TAP" four times, and then add the rhyme. Ask the children to suggest different places to tap, different ways (other than tapping) to keep the beat, or new verses (such as "**Ker**ry C. **dressed** in red, **Gol**den bows **on** her head…").

Variation

If you are working with 5- to 7-year-olds, ask them to sit in pairs, with one child behind the other. The child in back taps the shoulders of the one in front. The one in front says "TAP" with each tap. Establish a common beat for the class, and then add the rhyme. Then have each pair of children trade places, and repeat the rhyme.

Piggy on the Railroad

***Pig**gy on the **rail**road **bend**ing up and **down**,
A**long** came an **en**gine with **hard**ly any **sound**.
Piggy saw the **en**gine and **let** out a **cry**.
"You **real**ly shouldn't **play** here," said the **en**gine with a **sigh**.*

Category

Rhyme

Age

4–7

Equipment

None

Procedure

Ask the children to explore different ways to move their hands or arms, on one side at a time, to a slow beat. They might try hammering with one hand, patting with one hand, flapping one arm against the body, or shaking one hand. Identify what an individual child is doing, and ask that child to lead the group in doing his or her movement while the others imitate it. Everyone then can do the same motion on the other side of the body. The teacher chants the anchor word "BEAT" four times to the child's established beat. For the first line of the rhyme, ask everyone to use one arm or one hand to move to four slow beats, and then have them do the same thing, using the other arm or hand, for the second line of the rhyme. Repeat with the third and fourth lines. Invite another child to select the next movement, and have everyone practice it before adding the rhyme. It might be appropriate to discuss the rhyme with the children, noting Piggy's recklessness in playing by the tracks.

Slippery, Slimy, Gooey Mush

__Slush__ slush, __goo__ey mush,
__Slip__pery, slimy, __please__ don't rush;
__Just__ go slow.
__Don't__ you know that it's
__Slip__pery, slimy, __goo__ey mush.

Category

Rhyme

Age

5–7

Equipment

Two large grocery bags for each child (one bag for each foot)

Formation

Ask the children to scatter about the area so there is room to slide their feet around.

Procedure

Ask the children to think of ways to use the grocery bags to move around. Identify what one child is doing, and ask everyone to try it: "Adrienne has her feet inside the bags and is sliding with them. Let's do it her way." If no one thinks of putting bags on both feet, suggest that the children try this. Once they have mastered sliding around with the bags, establish a common beat and add the rhyme.

Variation

Instead of using bags to move around to the beat of this rhyme, children might pretend they are walking in pudding, or slushy snow, or anything else they can think of that is gooey and mushy.

Three Little Monkeys

__Three__ little __mon__keys __swing__ing in a __tree__,
A__long__ came a __croc__odile __qui__et as can __be__;
The __mon__keys __said__, "You __can't__ catch __me!__" SNAP.

Category

Rhyme

Age

5–7

Equipment

None

Formation

Ask the children to sit or stand in a circle.

Procedure

Show the children a picture of a crocodile, and ask them to show you how they think a crocodile snaps its jaws. Have the children do their imitations of the crocodile's bite as you say "SNAP." Explain that you will be introducing a rhyme about a crocodile that snaps its jaws in this way.

Next ask the children to think of different ways to swing their arms, legs, or combinations of the two. Choose one child's beat, and say "SWING" with each of the child's swinging movements. Ask the other children to say "SWING" with you and to swing the way the leader is swinging. When all are swinging together, add the rhyme. When the "SNAP" occurs, children can do their imitations of the crocodile snapping its jaws.

Variation

Divide the children into groups of three. Let each group choose the way they want to swing their arms or legs. Set the beat with the anchor word "SWING," and add the rhyme below, using all three verses. On the first "SNAP," one child in each group falls down. On the second "SNAP," a second child in the group falls down. After the third "SNAP," the third child says, "Missed me." Repeat the rhyme several times, so that each child has a chance to say "Missed me."

Three little monkeys swinging in a tree,
Along came a crocodile quiet as can be;
The first monkey said, "You can't catch me!" SNAP.

Two little monkeys swinging in a tree,
Along came a crocodile quiet as can be;
The second monkey said, "You can't catch me!" SNAP.

One little monkey swinging in a tree,
Along came a crocodile quiet as can be;
The last monkey said, "You can't catch me!" SNAP. "Missed me."

The Train Went Into the Tunnel

*The **train** went into the **tun**nel,*
*To **see** what it could **see**.*
*And **when** it came out of the **tun**nel,*
*It **moved** around like **me**.*

Category

Rhyme

Age

4–7

Equipment

A "tunnel" made of a large carton (appliance-sized) with a hole at each end, or a blanket over a table

Formation

Ask the children to stand in a circle (that includes the "tunnel").

Procedure

Have the children suggest different ways they might move around the circle and through the tunnel (for example, they might choose to shuffle, hop, or skip). After the group chooses one of these ways to move around the circle, begin a slow, steady beat, using "CHUG" as the anchor word, and then add the rhyme. At the end of the rhyme, the child who emerges from the tunnel on the word "me" chooses a different way for the children to move around the circle as the rhyme is repeated.

Variation

Have the children form "trains" by walking around in groups of four, with one child walking behind the other and each child holding onto the one in front of him or her. They say the rhyme while walking. On the word "me," the trains stop, and each train copies its leader's movements while all are standing in place. The leader then goes to the end of the line, and a new child is the leader.

Action Songs

All Around the Hula Hoop

(Pop Goes the Weasel)

Category

Action song

Age

4–7

Equipment

A hula hoop for each child (or one large circle marked on the floor)

Formation

Children stand either inside or outside their hoops (or the circle).

Procedure

Have the children explore ways of moving around the outside of their hula hoops. (If you use a large circle on the floor, ask some children to move around the inside of the circle while others move around the outside.) Encourage the children to talk about how they are moving and to try one another's ideas for moving. Identify, for example, one of the children who is jumping inside the hoop, and ask the rest of the children to imitate this jumping. You might make such comments as these: "Jacob says he is skipping around the circle; Erica, how are you moving? Robby is hopping around his hoop—let's try it his way." Next, tell them that the magic word is "POP," and when they hear it, that is the signal to stop the way they are moving and to jump inside their hoops. (When using a large circle, the children can jump in place.) Ask individual children to try saying the magic word as a signal for the other children to jump. Ask the children to begin moving around the outside of their hoops as you anchor the beat by saying some descriptive word, such as "SKIP," four times; then begin the song. Remind the children to listen for the signal to jump. Also, discuss how they might "freeze" when the song says "all freeze now."

All Around the Hula Hoop

Traditional tune

All a-round the hu- la hoop, The
child-ren now are walk- ing. The
child-ren thought it was all in fun.
pop and all freeze now.

Allison's Camel

Category

Action song

Age

5–7

Equipment

Pictures of camels with one to five humps and a picture of a camel with no humps (a horse)

Formation

Separate the children into groups of five, and have the children within each group stand so they are lined up one behind the other.

Procedure

First, show the children the pictures of the five-humped camel, the four-humped camel, and so on. As you go from picture to picture, encourage them to talk about what is happening to the camel's humps. Ask the children to do what you are doing as you pat your legs slowly. Say the anchor word "PAT" four times, and then add the song. Next, have each child hold onto both arms or both shoulders of the person in front of him or her and rock back and forth slowly. As the children rock in this way, you say "ROCK, ROCK" four times, and then repeat the song.

To perform the entire song, ask the standing children to rock while you sing the song, concluding with "Boom, boom, boom." This signals the first person in each group to sit down (which means that the camel loses one hump). As you repeat the song, the children who remain standing rock to the slow beat while the seated children rock and pat the slow beat on their legs. Next, show the picture of the camel with four humps, and repeat the song and the motions until the camel loses another hump. Continue in this way until all the children are seated. At the end of the song, show the picture of the camel with no hump (the horse).

Allison's Camel

Al-li-son's cam-el has five humps;

Al-li-son's cam-el has five humps;

Al-li-son's cam-el has five humps; so

go, Al-li-son, go.

Verse 2: Allison's camel has four humps...
Verse 3: Allison's camel has three humps...
Verse 4: Allison's camel has two humps...
Verse 5: Allison's camel has one hump...

Bend and Straighten Is the Game
(London Bridge Is Falling Down)

Category

Action song

Age

3–7

Equipment

None

Formation

Ask the children to sit in a circle.

Procedure

Ask the children to explore ways to bend and straighten different parts of their bodies. Encourage them to talk about what body parts they are using and how they are moving them. To prepare for the way the song ends, have them do one jump and then say their names. Establish the beat for the song by asking one child to lead by demonstrating one way of bending and straightening; have the other children imitate this leader. Reinforce their movements by saying "BEND" as they bend and "STRAIGHTEN" as they straighten. After repeating "BEND, STRAIGHTEN" four times, add the song. If the song's ending is too complicated for your group, try ending with "Bend and say your name" or "Now it's time to stop." Endings for older children might be "Jump and say your street (city, pet's, or friend's) name." Children might make up other verses ("Fast and slow . . . , Tall and short . . . , Loud and soft is the game"), and they might suggest different ways to end the song.

Bend and Straighten Is the Game

Bend and straight-en is the game, is the game, is the game.

Bend and straight-en is the game. Jump and say your name:

Charlie Turn Your Arm
(Charlie Over the Ocean)

Category

Action song

Age

4–7

Equipment

None

Formation

Ask the children to sit around the area.

Procedure

Explore different nonlocomotor movements with the children, such as swinging, twisting, turning, or rocking. Ask one child to lead by demonstrating a movement and describing it to the other children: "Marcus, I see that you're moving your arm. How are you moving it?" Have the other children imitate the movement, and then use that movement to establish the beat, using an anchor word that best describes the movement (for example, "TWIST" or "BOUNCE"). Add the song, substituting the leader's name for "Charlie." The leader performs the movement alone on the first and third lines ("Marcus turn your arm"), and the children join in on the second and fourth lines ("We can do it too").

Charlie Turn Your Arm

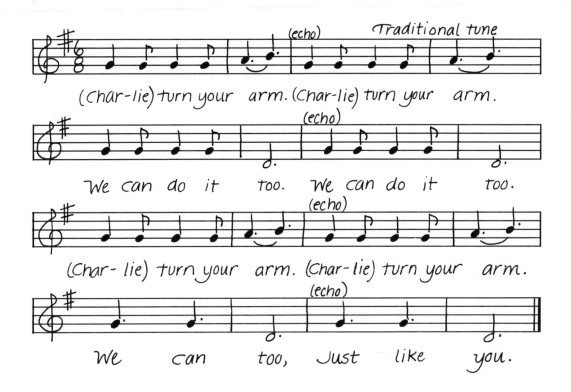

(Char-lie) turn your arm. (Char-lie) turn your arm.

We can do it too. We can do it too.

(Char-lie) turn your arm. (Char-lie) turn your arm.

We can too, Just like you.

Down by the Station

Category

Action song (modified version)

Age

4–7

Equipment

None

Formation

Ask the children to sit scattered around the area.

Procedure

Rock your body back and forth, and ask the children to describe what your body is doing. Ask them to try moving their bodies the same way. Once they are accustomed to the movement, say "CHOO" four times to anchor the beat, and then add the song. If you have a real whistle, use the whistle sound, rather than a word, to anchor the beat.

Variation

Once the children are familiar with the song, ask them to talk about ways they could pretend to be a train. Identify one child's idea and say "Let's line up the way Daniel suggested and try the song that way." Or ask the whole group to line up like one long train, and ask them to talk about the different parts of the train—"What are some of the cars on a train called? Oh, I see that Anna and Joe are the freight cars."

Down by the Station

Traditional tune

Down by the sta-tion, ear-ly in the morn-ing,

See the lit-tle puf-fer trains all in a row.

See the en-gine driv-er pull the lit-tle han-dle,
(blow the little whis-tle)

Choo, choo, choo, and off we go.
(Toot), (toot), (toot)

Everyone Keep the Beat
(Looby Loo)

Category

Action song

Age

3–7

Equipment

None

Formation

Have the children stand either in a circle or scattered around the area.

Procedure

Teach this song in two parts, the refrain first and then the verses. Ask a child to show you how to keep the beat (for example, by patting both knees), and have the other children copy the movement. Use "KNEES" or "PAT" as the anchor word, repeat it four times, and then add the refrain.

To prepare the children to learn the verses, ask them to think of a way to move both arms (in and out, up and down, for example). Describe what they are doing, and add the appropriate labels as the anchor words ("IN, OUT"; "UP, DOWN"; and so on): "Diane is stretching her arms over her head. Kevin, what are you doing with your arms?" Next, have them shake both hands in front of their bodies and then turn around. Repeat the sequence and add the verse. With each repetition, change the movement used to keep the beat in the refrain, and change the body part(s) used in the verse. Encourage the children to think of new verses and different ways to keep the beat.

Everyone Keep the Beat

Ev-'ry-one keep the beat. Ev-'ry-one keep the beat.

Ev-'ry-one keep the beat, All on a (Mon-day) morn-ing. We

put our two hands in. We put our two hands out. We

put our two hands in a-gain, And wig-gle our-selves a-bout.

Verse 2: We put our two hands up. We put our
Two hands down.
We give our two hands a shake, shake, shake,
And turn ourselves around.

Verse 3: We put our two hands together.
We put our two hands apart.
We give our two hands a shake, shake, shake,
And turn around for the start.

Gallop All Around

Category

Action song

Age

3–7

Equipment

None

Formation

Ask the children to stand scattered about the area.

Procedure

Ask the children to show you how they would gallop if they were horses. Then explain to them that at the end of the song, after they have galloped, you will name a part of the body and ask them to touch that body part to the floor ("Put your _____ on the ground"). Ask the children to start galloping, establish the beat by saying "GALLOP" four or eight times, and then start the song.

Variation

Ask the children to explore different kinds of locomotor movement, and encourage them to make up new verses by substituting different ways to move (skip, hop, crawl) or different body parts to "put on the ground."

Gallop All Around

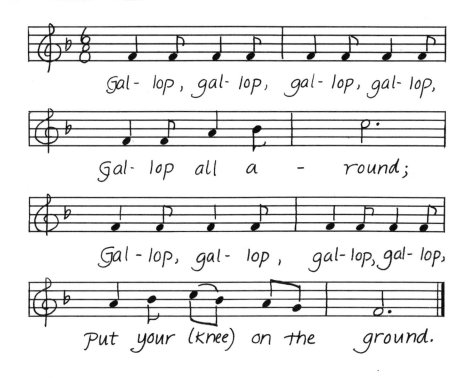

Gal- lop, gal- lop, gal- lop, gal- lop,

Gal- lop all a - round;

Gal- lop, gal- lop, gal- lop, gal- lop,

Put your (knee) on the ground.

Gonna Shake Out My Hands

Category

Action song

Age

3–7

Equipment

None

Formation

Have the children sit scattered around the area.

Procedure

Ask the children to shake their hands. Then ask them to describe where they are shaking them. Demonstrate the following sequence: Shake the hands in front of the body, then high, then low, then in front again. Begin the sequence with the children, and say "SHAKE, SHAKE" slowly four times; then add the song.

Variation

Form variations of the first verse by substituting "far" and "near," or "big" and "little," for "high" and "low."

Gonna Shake Out My Hands

Gon-na shake out my hands. Gon-na shake out my hands.

Shake 'em high, shake 'em low, Shake out my hands.

Verse 2:   Gonna wiggle my thumbs.
             Gonna wiggle my thumbs.
             Wiggle 'em up, wiggle 'em down,
             Wiggle my thumbs.
Verse 3:   Gonna dance with my fingers.
             Gonna dance with my fingers.
             Dance 'em up, dance 'em down,
             Dance with my fingers.

Hop, Everybody
(Hop, Old Squirrel)

Category

Action song

Age

4–7

Equipment

None

Formation

Ask the children to stand so they are scattered about the area. You may wish to define the space by giving each child a carpet square or hula hoop.

Procedure

Explore different locomotor movements with the children, such as stepping, marching, jumping, and jogging. Ask the children to try a movement, and encourage them to talk about it. Identify one child's movement, and have the other children copy it: "I see that Michael is hopping. Let's all try hopping." Use an anchor word, such as "HOP," four or eight times, and then add the song. Create new verses by asking the children to suggest other ways to move.

Hop, Everybody

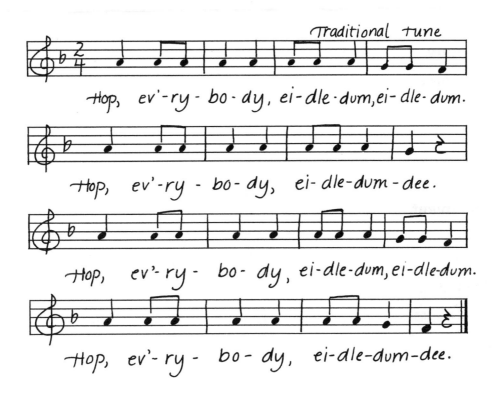

Traditional tune

Hop, ev'-ry-bo-dy, ei-dle-dum, ei-dle-dum.

Hop, ev'-ry-bo-dy, ei-dle-dum-dee.

Hop, ev'-ry-bo-dy, ei-dle-dum, ei-dle-dum.

Hop, ev'-ry-bo-dy, ei-dle-dum-dee.

I Can Move One Foot

(Pretty Trappings)

Category

Action song

Age

3–7

Equipment

None

Formation

Have the children sit in a circle.

Procedure

Show the children how you can move one foot without moving the other, and then ask them to do what you are doing. Then switch feet, and do the same thing. Next ask a child to volunteer to be the leader in moving one foot without moving the other. Establish the child's beat by repeating the anchor word "FOOT" four times, and then start the song. After singing Verses 1 and 2, encourage children to suggest new verses using other "paired" parts of the body.

I Can Move One Foot

Traditional tune

I can move one foot, but the o-ther's good for no-thing. I can move one foot, but the o-ther is no good.

Verse 2: I can move the other foot, but
the first one's good for nothing.
I can move the other foot, but
the first one is no good.

Johnny, Pat Your Knees

(Johnny, Get Your Hair Cut)

Category

Action song

Age

3–7

Equipment

None

Formation

Ask the children to sit in a circle.

Procedure

Begin by asking the children to find places to pat, either on their bodies or nearby on the floor. Encourage a child to be the leader, and use an anchor word that corresponds to the place that the child is patting, such as "KNEES" or "FLOOR." Repeat the anchor word four or eight times before starting the song. Substitute the leader's name for "Johnny."

Johnny Pat Your Knees

(John-ny), pat your knees, knees, knees.

(John-ny), pat your knees just like this.

Let Everyone Keep the Beat

(Let Everyone Clap Hands With Me)

Category

Action song

Age

3–7

Equipment

None

Formation

Have the children sit or stand around the area.

Procedure

Ask a child to lead the activity either by patting the beat on a body part or by swinging both arms, shaking both hands, twisting both arms. Have everyone copy the leader, and then anchor the beat with a word that describes the movement. Repeat this four or eight times, and then begin the song. Each time the song is repeated, have a different child select the movement.

Let Everyone Keep the Beat

Folk song

Let ev'-ry one keep the beat. Let ev'-ry one keep the beat. Come on now join in-to the game. You'll find that it's al-ways the same!

Monster, Monster, Monster Man

(Row, Row, Row Your Boat)

Category

Action song

Age

5–7

Equipment

None

Formation

Ask the children to stand so they are scattered about the area and have room to move.

Procedure

Talk with the children about Halloween monsters, pumpkins (jack-o-lanterns), ghosts, witches, and skeletons. Ask the children to think about how each of these Halloween characters might move, and encourage them to explore these movements. Identify what individual children are doing: "I see that Ivan is walking like a scary monster. Are there other ways to move like a monster?" Ask for a leader to choose a Halloween character and a way for that character to move, and use the name for that movement as the anchor word, repeating it four or eight times before adding the song. Choose a new leader for each verse, and encourage the children to think of new verses.

Monster, Monster, Monster Man

Mon-ster, mon-ster, mon-ster man, Walk a-round the space.

Oo __ Oo __ Oo __ Oo __ It's a sca-ry place.

Verse 2: Pumpkin, pumpkin, pumpkin bright,
          Roll around the space.
Verse 3: Ghost, ghost, goblin ghost,
          Float around the space.
Verse 4: Witches, witches on your brooms,
          Gallop 'round the space.
Verse 5: Boney, boney, boney man,
          Hop around the space.

My Bonnie Lies Over the Ocean

Category

Action song

Age

6–7

Equipment

For each child, a capped plastic milk jug partially filled with water that's tinted with blue food coloring

Formation

Ask the children to spread out around the area.

Procedure

Talk with the children about oceans and other large bodies of water. Encourage them to talk about experiences they have had swimming or playing by the water. Next, hold onto the two ends of the jug, and tip it to and fro (like a steering wheel). As the children watch what you are doing, ask them to describe the movement, and have them try to tip their jugs in this way. When they are comfortable with this, set the beat by saying an anchor word (such as "SLOSH" or "SPLASH") four or eight times, and then start the song. As you sing the chorus, "Bring back, bring back . . . ," move the jug away from and towards your body. You can repeat the song several times, substituting the children's names for "Bonnie."

My Bonnie Lies Over the Ocean

Traditional tune

My Bon-nie lies o-ver the o-cean. My

Bon-nie lies o-ver the sea. My

Bon-nie lies o-ver the o-cean. Oh,

bring back my Bon-nie to me.

Bring back, bring back, Oh, bring back my Bon-nie to

me, to me. Bring back, bring back, Oh,

bring back my Bon-nie to me.

My Hands Keep Moving

Category

Action song

Age

3–7

Equipment

None

Formation

Have the children stand or sit in a circle.

Procedure

Begin the song by asking the children to think of a way to move their hands. Ask for a volunteer to be the leader, and have the other children copy the leader's movements. "Mark is moving his arms around and around. Let's do it his way." Select an anchor word (for example, "MOVE" or "ROUND"), repeat it four or eight times to establish a common beat, and then add the song. Encourage the children to make up new verses by substituting different body parts and different movements.

My Hands Keep Moving

All day my hands keep mo-ving, keep mo-ving, keep mo-ving. All
day my hands keep mo-ving, 'round and 'round like this.

Verse 2: All day my body keeps bouncing...
          up and down like this.
Verse 3: All day my arms keep swinging...
          back and forth like this.
Verse 4: All day my feet keep walking...
          step and step like this.
Verse 5: All day my legs keep marching...
          march and march like this.

Number One

Category

Action song

Age

3–7

Equipment

None

Formation

Have the children sit or stand in a circle.

Procedure

Start tapping your knees, and ask the children to do what you do. Encourage them to find different places to tap, and then ask them to think of a way to change their taps: "Can you tap slowly? Quickly? Heavy taps? Light taps?" Ask one child to be the leader, and have the others copy the leader's tapping beat. Use a descriptive anchor word, such as "TAP," and repeat it four or eight times; then add the song. For the next verse, encourage the children to find their own place to tap. Ask the children for help in developing new verses.

Number One

verse   British folk tune

Num-ber one, num-ber one, now my beat has

Chorus

just be-gun, With a rum tum tad-dle - um,

rum tum tad-dle-um, rum tum tad-dle-um Tum.

Verse 2: Number two, number two, let us
see what we can do.

Verse 3: Number three, number three, pat
the beat upon your knee.

Verse 4: Number four, number four, see if
you can tap the floor.

Our Fingers and Thumbs Keep Moving

(One Finger, One Thumb)

Category

Action song

Age

3–7

Equipment

None

Formation

Have the children sit or stand in a circle.

Procedure

Ask the children to show you how they can make their fingers and thumbs move. Then use an anchor word, such as "FINGERS" or "THUMBS," to set the beat for their movement of fingers and thumbs. Repeat the anchor word four or eight times, and then add the song. Encourage the children to make up succeeding verses by adding a new body part to the ones in the previous verse.

Our Fingers and Thumbs Keep Moving

Our fin-gers and thumbs keep mo-ving. Our fin-gers and thumbs keep mo-ving. Our fin-gers and thumbs keep mo-ving. They're mo-ving and then they stop.

Verse 2: Our fingers and thumbs and arms keep moving...

Verse 3: Our fingers and thumbs and arms and legs keep moving...

59

Pat Your Chin and Not Your Hair

(Jimmy Crack Corn)

Category

Action song

Age

4–7

Equipment

None

Formation

Ask the children to sit or stand around the area.

Procedure

Ask the children to watch what you are doing and to join in with you when they are ready to do so. Start patting your chin slowly, repeat the anchor word "PAT" four or eight times, and then start the song. Add new verses by asking the children to suggest new places to pat.

Pat Your Chin and Not Your Hair

Pat your chin and not your hair. Pat your chin and not your hair.

Pat your chin and not your hair. Pat it a-gain and now stop!

Verse 2: One hand up in the air,
Other hand up in the air,
Both hands up in the air,
Bring them down, and pat your knees!

Ritsch, Ratsch

Category

Action song

Age

3–7

Equipment

None

Formation

Have the children sit in a circle.

Procedure

Begin by pounding your fists on your upper legs, using a slow steady beat, or ask one of the children to set the beat in this way. Anchor the leader's beat by saying "BOOM" four times, and then add the song. Ask the children to choose other places to pound their fists or other ways to keep the beat.

Ritsch, Ratsch

Ritsch, ratsch, fi-li- boom, boom, boom, fi-li-

boom, boom, boom, fi-li- boom, boom, boom.

Ritsch, ratsch, fi-li- boom, boom, boom, fi-li

boom, boom, boom, fi-li- boom, boom, boom.

Row, Row, Row Your Boat

Category

Action song

Age

3–7

Equipment

None

Formation

Have the children either sit in a circle or sit one behind the other, in short lines.

Procedure

Ask the children to move their bodies as if they were in a boat. Describe what they are doing: "Laura, you're rocking back and forth. What kind of a boat are you in?" Then, "Let's pretend we are all in Laura's rowboat. How should we move?" Select an anchor word that describes the movement, and repeat it four times. Then start the song. To add new verses, ask the children to think of other kinds of boats and to describe how they would move (paddle, steer, sail) down the stream.

Row, Row, Row Your Boat

Row, row, row your boat, Gent-ly down the stream.

Mer-ri-ly, mer-ri-ly, mer-ri-ly, mer-ri-ly, Life is but a dream.

Shake to My Lou

(Skip to My Lou)

Category

Action song

Age

3–7

Equipment

None

Formation

Ask all the children to sit or to stand in an informal circle.

Procedure

Start by asking the children to shake both hands in front of their bodies. Then suggest that they find other places to shake their hands, such as up in the air, down low, or to one side. Ask one child to be the leader, and have the other children follow the leader's movement. Once the children begin, chant "SHAKE" four times to the leader's beat, and then start the song. (If the leader is doing the movement too quickly, suggest that the shaking be a little slower.)

Variation

Encourage the children to suggest other anchor words (and movements) to use for the song, such as "PAT" (pat any body part), "BOUNCE" (pretend to bounce a ball), "PUSH" (push both arms in any direction), "FLAP" (flap both arms like a chicken), "JIGGLE" (jiggle the whole body), "MARCH" (march in place), "JUMP," or "HOP."

Shake to My Lou

Traditional tune

Shake, shake, shake to my Lou, Shake, shake, shake to my Lou,

Shake, shake, shake to my Lou, Shake to my Lou and now stop.
(my dar-ling).

Sing, Sing Together

Category

Action song

Age

5–7

Equipment

One pair of rhythm sticks for each child

Formation

Have the children sit in a circle.

Procedure

Show the children how to tap their knees slowly with the rhythm sticks, saying "KNEES" with each tap. Then have them try slowly hitting the sticks together overhead, saying "HIT" each time the sticks come together. Combine the two parts, using four beats for each type of movement. Next, tap the floor once, saying "FLOOR," and then hit the sticks together once, saying "HIT" (this "FLOOR, HIT" part is performed twice). Have the children practice this last sequence several times.

Finally, put the entire sequence together, using *all* the anchor words— "KNEES, KNEES, KNEES, KNEES, HIT, HIT, HIT, HIT, FLOOR, HIT, FLOOR, HIT," and then add the song. The first line of the song goes with the knee taps, the second line goes with the sticks hitting overhead, and the last line goes with the floor-overhead, floor-overhead sequence.

Variation

Rock or sway while singing the song, changing the words to fit the movement you have chosen (for example, change the words to "Rock, rock together . . .").

Sing, Sing Together

Sing, sing to-geth-er, mer-ri-ly, mer-ri-ly sing.

Sing, sing to-geth-er, mer-ri-ly, mer-ri-ly sing.

Sing, sing, sing, sing.

Special Place

(Here We Go 'Round the Mulberry Bush)

Category

Action song

Age

4–7

Equipment

A hula hoop for each child

Formation

Have the children stand scattered about the area, inside their hula hoops.

Procedure

Begin by encouraging the children to move around inside their hoops and to talk about how they are moving. Sing the song while they are moving. The second time you sing the song, try establishing the beat with a sound, such as the sound of a drum or of some other instrument. If a child acts as leader in moving around his or her hoop, then establish the child's beat with an appropriate word, such as "WALK" or "HOP," repeating it four or eight times.

For the second verse, one child can "freeze" in position while the others copy that child's "statue." The action song is continued by alternating statue copying with moving about inside the hula hoops.

Special Place

Go a-round your spe-cial place, your spe-cial place, your
spe-cial place. Go a-round your spe-cial place then you rest.

Verse 2: Match the statue that you see, that you see,
          that you see.
          Match the statue that you see. Then you go.

Swing Your Arms

(Row, Row, Row Your Boat)

Category

Action song

Age

3–7

Equipment

A carpet square or hula hoop for each child

Formation

Have the children form an informal circle, each standing on a carpet square or inside a hula hoop.

Procedure

Ask the children to watch what you do and then to do the same. Start by swinging both your arms to the back and to the front. After the children begin, stop your movements, so the children alone are swinging their arms. Ask them to describe where their arms are swinging. Have one child be the leader who starts to swing both arms as you chant "SWING" to the child's beat. Say the anchor word once as the arms go in back and again as the arms go in front. After saying the word four times, begin the song.

Variation

Encourage the children to suggest other ways to move their arms, and repeat the song, beginning each time by establishing the beat with the anchor word. Have the children suggest other anchor words (and ways to move), such as "TWIST" (twisting arms, legs, trunk), "TURN" (making circles with both arms or with one leg at a time), or "FLAP" (flapping the arms like a chicken). Have the children talk about the ways they are moving.

Swing Your Arms

Swing, swing, swing your arms. Swing them back and forth.

Swing, swing, swing your arms. Swing them both and stop.

Verse 2: Turn, turn, turn your arm.
Turn it all around.
Turn, turn, turn your arm.
Turn it now and stop.

This Is What I Can Do

Category

Action song

Age

3–7

Equipment

None

Formation

Have the children sit or stand in a circle.

Procedure

Ask the children to each move some body part. As they are moving, describe what individual children are doing: "I see that Athi is bending and straightening his knees. Let's all try doing that." Establish the beat by repeating an anchor word, such as "KNEES," four times; then begin the song. At the end of the song, you might choose a new leader by substituting a child's name in the last line of the song, in place of "you."

This Is What I Can Do

This is what I can do. See if you can do it too.

This is what I can do. Now I'll pass it on to you!

Tommy Thumb

Category

Action song

Age

4–7

Equipment

None

Formation

Have the children stand or sit around the area.

Procedure

Tell the children that you are going to play follow the leader and that they should do what you do. Put your thumbs up, put your thumbs down, and then say to the children "Think of ways to make your thumbs dance." Tap your thumbs on your shoulders two times slowly, on your head two times slowly, and on your knees two times slowly; then fold your arms. Repeat the sequence of movements without the song, and see if the children can follow you. Once they are comfortable with the movements, start the song. Ask them to recall where they tapped with their thumbs first, next, and last. Add new verses by using other fingers, all the fingers, two arms, or one arm and then the other arm.

Tommy Thumb

Tom-my Thumb is up and Tom-my Thumb is down.

Tom-my Thumb is danc-ing all a- round the town.

Dance him on your shoul-ders. Dance him on your head.

Dance him on your knees, and tuck him in-to bed.

Verse 2: Put your two arms up, and put
your two arms down.
Make your two arms do a dance
all around the town.
Straighten them in front, and straighten
them in back.
Bend them to the sides, and now you
lay them flat.

Walk Around the Chairs Today

(Mary Had a Little Lamb)

Category

Action song

Age

4–7

Equipment

A chair, a hula hoop, or a carpet square for each child

Formation

The children stand scattered about the space, each by a chair (hula hoop, carpet square).

Procedure

Ask the children to move in some way, going several times around their own chairs (hoops, squares), and to then sit down. Next have them explore other ways of going around their chairs, and encourage them to talk about the different ways they are moving. Ask for a volunteer to be the leader, and have the leader tell the other children how he or she is going to move around the chair. The leader starts the movement, and the other children copy. Have them repeat this while you use the anchor word to establish a beat that matches the leader's beat. Ask the children to suggest other types of movement, and substitute in the song a word appropriate for each of those movements.

Variation

Have school-aged children move around in the whole space, and at the end of the song, have them sit on any nearby chair. Revise the song accordingly: "Walk around the space with me. . . . Now all find a chair."

Walk Around the Chairs Today

Walk a-round the chairs to-day, chairs to-day, chairs to-day

Walk a-round the chairs to-day. Now we all sit down.

We Can Keep a Steady Beat
(Muffin Man)

Category

Action song

Age

3–7

Equipment

None

Formation

Children sit or stand in a circle.

Procedure

Prepare the children for this song by playing follow the leader, with children taking turns being the leader. The leader chooses a place to put both hands—for example, both hands on the knees—and waits for everyone to copy this movement. The leader can then ask the other children to identify where they have just put their hands. Each leader chooses a different location for the hands.

After the follow-the-leader game, ask the children to pat their knees, for example, and set the group beat by saying "KNEES" four times. Then add the first verse of the song. The child you name at the end of the first verse becomes the leader in patting some part of the body as the second verse is sung, and so on.

We Can Keep a Steady Beat

We can keep a stea-dy beat, a stea-dy beat, a stea-dy beat.

We can keep a stea-dy beat. (Con-nie) find the next place.

Verse 2: (Connie) keeps a steady beat, a steady
beat, a steady beat.
(Connie) keeps a steady beat. (Eric)
find the next place.

We Walk Our Feet

Category

Action song

Age

4–7

Equipment

None

Formation

Have the children stand in a circle.

Procedure

Ask the children to walk around the space and to explore different ways to place their feet as they walk. Talk about the way individual children are walking: "I see that Kestin is walking with her toes pointing in. Can you think of other things to do with your feet while you walk?" Identify one child's movement, and ask the children to imitate it. Matching the leader's beat, repeat an anchor word four or eight times, and then start the song. Instead of the phrase "toes in," subsequent verses might use "toes out," "big steps," "tiptoe," and so on.

We Walk Our Feet

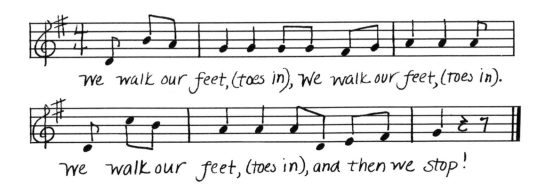

We walk our feet, (toes in), We walk our feet, (toes in).

We walk our feet, (toes in), and then we stop!

Yellow Bug

Category

Action song

Age

4–7

Equipment

For each child, two bugs that the child has made from a variety of teacher-provided materials (after a discussion about different kinds of bugs—how they look, move, and sound)

Procedure

Have everyone hold a bug in each hand. Ask the children to watch you and to do what you do. Move the bugs to different places on your body, such as on your head, on your knees, or in front of your body. Encourage the children to take turns being the leader and discovering new places for the bugs to go. Using the bugs to keep the beat, chant "BUG" four or eight times, and then start the song. At the end of the song, the leader places the bugs in a special place, and the rest of the children copy.

Variation

Encourage individual children to think of different ways to move the bugs at the end of the song. The last line can then be "What do you think that _____ (child's name) will do?" or "We know where _____'s (child's name) bugs will go." Create additional verses by asking the children to think of different colors that the bug could be.

Yellow Bug

Singing game

See the lit-tle yel-low bugs.

They live un-der the yel-low rug.

Where do you think that they will go?

Notes